FACING DIVORCE

IN NEW YORK

GUIDE TO SURVIVING DIVORCE, CHILD CUSTODY, CHILD SUPPORT AND SPOUSAL MAINTENANCE

By Elliot S. Schlissel, Esq.

ISBN: 978-1-941645-05-5

Design and Published by:

Speakeasy Marketing, Inc.
73-03 Bell Blvd #10
Oakland Gardens, N.Y. 11364
www.SpeakeasyMarketingInc.com

888-225-8594

DISCLAIMER

This publication is intended to be informational only. No legal advice is being given, and no attorney-client relationship is intended to be created by reading this material. If you are facing legal issues, whether criminal or civil, seek professional legal counsel to get your questions answered.

Law Office of Elliot S. Schlissel

479 Merrick Road

Lynbrook, NY 11563

(516) 561-6645

(718) 350-2802

Schlissel.law@att.net

www.schlissellawfirm.com

Client Testimonials

"Elliot Schlissel assisted me through a divorce and made it as painless as could be. He has an excellent ability to break down the legal system and explain it in a way that people can easily comprehend. He applied the law to my case while constantly encouraging my feedback to ensure the case was resolved in a manner I was happy with and was favorable to my circumstances. I would recommend him for anyone in need of legal services."

- A Divorce Client.

....

"Great Divorce Attorney. My experience with the Law Office of Elliot Schlissel has met all of my legal needs. Mr. Schlissel provided me with information concerning my family issues in a timely manner. A convenient appointment was set up and I was seen shortly after by Mr. Schlissel at his office. I am very pleased with the results on my case." **- A Divorce Client.**

....

TABLE OF CONTENTS

ATTORNEY INTRODUCTION

Attorney Elliot S. Schlissel has been practicing law for more than 36 years. He attended SUNY at Buffalo Law School. He received a scholarship to study international protection of human rights at the Council of Europe in Strasbourg, France.

Attorney Schlissel is currently a member of the New York State Bar Association, Nassau County Bar Association, Queens County Bar Association and Suffolk County Bar Association. He served two terms as the President of the Commercial Lawyers Conference of New York, a regional bar association.

His goal is to provide his clients with high quality and cost effective legal services. Attorney Schlissel believes in treating each client, small or large, with dignity and rendering the professional, efficient and courteous service they deserve.

There are certain events in everyone's life that are recognized as being very stressful; A divorce, a custody dispute, child visitation issues, a parent relocating with the children, child support issues and financial issues in divorce proceedings . These are the times when it is necessary to enlist the services of an experienced lawyer.

Attorney Schlissel seeks to make the legal process less confusing and less stressful.

GENDER DIFFERENCE IN DIVORCE PROCESS

Interviewer: Do you see that men versus women view the divorce process differently?

Elliot S. Schlissel: Yes. Men feel they're discriminated against and that even though the law is gender neutral the judges in many situations seem to favor mothers.

Interviewer: What about women? How do they feel about it?

Elliot S. Schlissel: Women feel courts are not responsive enough to their needs. They act too slowly. They also feel they re not protected by the legal system with regard to their financial needs and needs involving domestic violence.

No-Fault Divorce in New York

Interviewer: Over the years that you've been practicing, have you seen that divorce has evolved and changed? Do people talk differently about it today than they used to talk?

Elliot S. Schlissel: Yes. Up until a few years ago, you had to prove, in the state of New York either, adultery, cruel inhuman treatment, living apart under written agreement of separation, or abandonment to get a divorce. It changed in 2010 and a "no-fault" divorce law was passed in New York. Now all you have to show is that there has been irretrievable breakdown of the relationship for a period of more than six months and the parties can get a divorce.

The irretrievable breakdown does not have to be spelled out. You just basically have to state, in the legal documents, "The marital relationship has broken down for six months, so I want a divorce," and you can get a divorce. The court then focuses on issues involving child custody, child support, spousal maintenance, division of property, and other issues related to the financial circumstances of the divorce.

Common Reasons for Divorce

Interviewer: When people come to you and they want a divorce, what's the most common reason that they give you?

Elliot S. Schlissel: Well, the most common reason is unhappiness in their marital relationship. The derivation of the unhappiness can relate to adultery, financial circumstances, inattentiveness and a variety of other circumstances, but generally speaking, people get divorced because for one reason or another they're unhappy with their spouse and their marital circumstances.

CLIENT EMOTIONALITY & INTENT

Interviewer: When people come to you, emotionally do they want to tear the other person apart or do they just want to go peacefully? What do people tell you?

Elliot S. Schlissel:

Sometimes people tell me they want to punish their spouse for mental cruelty, physical cruelty, or sleeping around. Sometimes they want to get divorced amicably. I remind them that the purpose of divorce courts is not to punish their spouse or allow them to get even with their spouse.

The goal of the legal system regarding divorces and family law issues is to do what's fair and equitable pursuant to the New York Equitable Distribution Law and fair and equitable with regard to child support, spousal maintenance, visitation and custody issues. The law isn't designed for one spouse to punish the other spouse through the legal system.

Interviewer: If a client comes in and they're out to punish the other person, do you follow the client's wishes or do you tell them it doesn't really work that way and encourage them to go a more amicable route and try to work things out?

Elliot S. Schlissel: I explain to them the more amicable route is generally the less expensive and less stressful way to go. However, if the case can't be handled amicably and a tough position needs to be taken, my office takes an extremely aggressive position in defending our client's rights.

Contested v. Uncontested Divorce Timeframe

Interviewer: What happens if one person doesn't want a divorce and they say, "I'm not signing anything," and they refuse to cooperate with the proceeding?

Elliot S. Schlissel: In New York, since we now have a new no-fault law, the divorce is guaranteed whether the other side cooperates or not. However, the lack of cooperation can cause the case to be a more complicated contested litigation. In the contested divorce situations, it usually takes longer and costs the clients more money.

Interviewer: How long might an uncontested divorce take versus a contested one?

Elliot S. Schlissel: An uncontested divorce can take as little as three to six months and a contested divorce can take several years.

Interviewer: Does the place where a divorce is filed also impact on how long it can take?

Elliot S. Schlissel: That's correct. How long a divorce takes also is dependent on which county the divorce is filed in. My office represents clients in divorces in the five boroughs of the City of New York County, Nassau County, Suffolk County and Westchester County. In some counties, the courts are more efficient than other counties. In some counties, there are greater backlogs in the divorce courts than there are in other counties.

COMMON MISCONCEPTIONS REGARDING DIVORCE

Interviewer: What misconceptions do people have when they first come to speak to you?

Elliot S. Schlissel: There are many misconceptions concerning divorces. One of the misconceptions I hear is the parties have to live separately for a year prior to getting a divorce or they need  a separation agreement prior to getting divorced. That is not true. Another misconception is that fathers believe mothers will always get custody and they're never going to get custody, and that's also not true.

A misconception mothers sometimes have is that they are automatically entitled to sole custody of the parties'children. There may be a bias in their favor but mothers' getting sole custody of their children is not guaranteed.

It is important to understand there are many issues involved in divorces people often don't take into consideration. The division of assets in a divorce involves all assets. Hidden assets or assets which aren't right in front of people involve pensions, 401(k) plans, 403(b) plans and Individual Retirement Acts (IRAs). Spouses are entitled to a portion of the other party's deferred compensation plan, pension, IRAs and 401 (k) plans that accrued during the course of the marriage.

Professional Degrees & Licenses as Assets

Interviewer: So all assets that someone has acquired while married would be equitably divided?

Elliot S. Schlissel: Except for certain limited exceptions, that is correct. Now another asset people don't think can be divided are degrees and licenses. Medical licenses, medical degrees, law school licenses, law school degrees, accounting licenses, teaching licenses, bachelor's degrees, and master's degrees that are received during the marriage are actually a type of marital property subject to equitable distribution. Experts are hired to value the increased earning potential related to these degrees and licenses, and the other spouse is entitled to a portion of the enhanced earning potential.

Interviewer: Let's say someone has a medical license. How have you seen the courts value it?

Elliot S. Schlissel: I've seen medical degrees and medical licenses valued anywhere from about $300,000 to $800,000 for some specialties, and between $1,000,000 to $2,500,000 for other specialties.

Interviewer: I guess it causes one party to pay more in spousal maintenance, right?

Elliot S. Schlissel: Actually, you pay more equitable distribution related to the enhanced earning due to the license or degree earned during the marriage. Let's take a hypothetical. Let's say a medical license that was received during the marriage is worth a million dollars. In most situations, the spouse does not usually get fifty percent of the value because the person obtaining the license did the work in medical school and is working and providing the medical services to the patients he or she sees. Unless the spouse helped pay for the license, the spouse will usually receive between ten and twenty five percent of the value of the license.

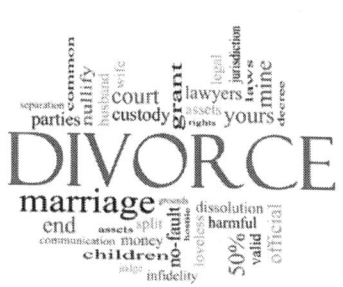

Interviewer: That would skew the distribution of everything else, but say there's a medical license involved as well as a house. That would place a heavy financial burden on the doctor to pay his/her spouse their equitable share of the license. What if the doctor doesn't have that much cash lying around?

Elliot S. Schlissel: There can be a trade-off, so let's say, in my example, a license is worth a million dollars and the spouse is going to receive a $150,000 – fifteen percent. There could be a trade-off of another asset worth a $150,000 such as a marital home or else the person who has the license would have to pay the spouse over time a $150,000.

ROLE OF AN ATTORNEY IN THE DIVORCE PROCESS

Interviewer: In a divorce, do both parties need to have their own separate attorney or can one attorney work with both people?

Elliot S. Schlissel: It is considered unethical for one attorney to represent two people in a divorce. It's considered a conflict of interest. It is possible to do a divorce with one attorney, but in that case the attorney would represent one party and the other party would represent himself or herself.

Interviewer: Once an attorney or two attorneys have been hired, are the husband and wife allowed to talk to each other? Are they encouraged to talk to each other or does everything go through the attorneys?

Elliot S. Schlissel: They can talk to each other; there's no rule against it. Sometimes it's even helpful if they are amicable and reasonable with each other. If they don't get along and there's hostility, the attorneys usually suggest the communication go through the lawyers.

The Mediation Process in New York

Interviewer: What about Mediation, is it available in New York?

Elliot S. Schlissel: Yes and one of my associate attorneys is a mediator. We do mediation in the office. In mediation situations, usually, neither party is represented by an attorney during the process. The mediator acts as a neutral party to facilitate communication between the parties so they can amicably resolve the various issues in the divorce. The mediator then drafts an agreement based on what the parties decided. Once signed by both parties, the mediation agreement resolves all the issues in a divorce situation.

Interviewer: What circumstances would you recommend mediation versus divorce or vice versa?

Elliot S. Schlissel: Mediation works when the issues are not very complicated. It helps if the parties are both reasonable people interested in compromising and amicably working issues out. Mediation tends to be successful if the level of tension and anger between the parties is minimal.

Advice to Clients

Interviewer: To help your client get though the divorce process, do you have any recommendations while their case is ongoing? Should they start budgeting differently? Should they make plans to look forward to where they're going to live?

Elliot S. Schlissel: Yes, no matter which party you are, a divorce will have financial implications for you.

Interviewer: Any advice you give clients to help prepare them for the difficulties they face in the divorce process?

Elliot S. Schlissel: I sometimes tell clients it's like getting sick and going to a doctor. Sometimes the prescribed antibiotic makes you feel a little sicker before it helps you recover. Sometimes, in divorces, to resolve the matter the heat gets turned up a bit before things eventually are resolved.

Interviewer: That's necessary?

Elliot S. Schlissel: In some situations it is. You have to make a point you're going to stand up for your rights and not be taken advantage of. If your spouse is not acting in an appropriate manner or is not amicable or willing to be fair and reasonable you have to make it clear that he or she is not going to get away with it. You should be fair and reasonable but not a pushover.

Annulments

Interviewer: Do you ever have people calling you asking you for annulments?

Elliot S. Schlissel: Yes, we do a lot of uncontested annulments. People are unaware annulments are becoming more and more common in the state of New York. The usual ground for an annulment is called "fraud in the inducement". It basically means your spouse made a representation to you prior to the marriage and you relied on that representation when you married them

Most of the annulments I do are uncontested, i.e. both parties agree to it. Therefore as far as the court goes, one party doesn't have to admit or deny the allegation of fraud. He or she just consents to the annulment neither admitting nor denying the allegations.

Interviewer: Can you give one example of a very common reason to seek an annulment?

Elliot S. Schlissel: A common example in the metropolitan New York area involves one party charming the other party into getting married and really only getting married for the purpose of getting a green card or immigration status in the United States. Another significant reason for annulments has to do with a prior financial history, i.e. representing you have lots of money and then turning out to be in debt up to your ears.

Other examples of what can serve as a basis for obtaining an annulment are people not advising their spouse of prior marriages, prior times they've served in prison, prior family-related illnesses, inherited types of illnesses or refusal to have children.

Spousal Maintenance

Interviewer: Well, let's talk about alimony or spousal maintenance. What's it called in New York?

Elliot S. Schlissel: The money one spouse pays to another spouse after the divorce is finalized is referred to as spousal maintenance. Spousal maintenance is the legally correct term for what used to be called alimony. It's the more modern term. You can only obtain spousal maintenance in the state of New York if you are actually married. Couples living together are unable to obtain spousal maintenance.

Interviewer: Is there common law marriage in New York?

Elliot S. Schlissel: New York is a state that does not recognize common law marriage. You can live with your boyfriend or girlfriend for twenty-five years or more and you will still be considered not married in the eyes of the law.

There Are Two Types of Spousal Maintenance in New York

Interviewer: In general, how does spousal maintenance work? Does it look just at the relative income of the two parties?

Elliot S. Schlissel: A spouse can be ordered to pay a monthly amount to the other under two separate headings. There are two types of spousal maintenance in the state of  New York. One is "spousal support" or "temporary spousal maintenance" which is the monthly money paid during the pendency of the divorce proceeding and the other is "spousal maintenance" which is paid after the parties get divorced. The issues in spousal maintenance are how much the moneyed spouse will pay to the non-moneyed spouse and for how long. Sometimes spousal maintenance is rehabilitative to allow the non-moneyed spouse to be retrained to get back into the workforce. Sometimes, it's paid for a period of time to supplement his or her income while he or she becomes self supporting.

The amount of money and the duration of time the spousal maintenance is paid whether it be for one year, two years, three years, or the rest of their life is dependent on the facts and circumstances in each individual case.

Interviewer: What kinds of factors are in play?

Elliot S. Schlissel: There are numerous factors that are taken into consideration regarding spousal maintenance.

Interviewer: Let's just talk about maybe the top two or three factors that affect it.

Elliot S. Schlissel: Well, the length of the marriage, the earning potential of the two spouses, the health of the spouses, and whether the requesting spouse gave up a career to raise children or to promote the career of the other, are all significant factors.

Interviewer: Can a young woman marry some old rich guy and then divorce him after six months and take all of his money or get him to pay her lifetime maintenance?

Elliot S. Schlissel: That is a myth. When one party to the marriage is older and the other party is younger they're referred to as May/December marriages and a six-month marriage in your example would only involve potential spousal maintenance for a very short period of time reflecting the fact that it was a short marriage. The wife would also probably not be very successful with any other claim for the old man's property as he acquired it long before meeting her and she had little to do with his financial status during the past six months.

Interviewer: Any other myths surrounding spousal maintenance that you commonly hear?

Elliot S. Schlissel: The idea that people are supposed to be able to maintain the exact standard of living maintained during the marriage. In most marriages, people spend all of the money they earn on necessary life expenses and there is not a lot of surplus money. When they go from one household to two households, there may not be enough money to support both households at the same standard of living the parties enjoyed when they lived as a couple.

Generally in a marriage that ends in a divorce, unless both parties are independently employed and able to support themselves, someone's standard of living is likely going to go down.

The Formulas to Calculate Child Support

Interviewer: Is there a level to which the Child Support can go, percentage-wise of someone's income? Is there a limit to it?

Elliot S. Schlissel: With regard to child support, the support payments are seventeen percent of gross wages – less FICA [Federal Insurance Contributions Act] – and also deducting New York City income taxes if applicable,

for one child, twenty-five percent for two children, twenty-nine percent for three children and thirty-one percent for four children and no less than thirty five percent for five or more children.

Interviewer: What are the tax implications of spousal maintenance?

Elliot S. Schlissel: Spousal maintenance is taxable income to the person who receives the money and is a tax-deductible item for the person who pays the money. Attorneys take this into consideration when they're negotiating terms of spousal maintenance.

Interviewer: Can the court order a spousal maintenance award that will leave the payer destitute?

Elliot S. Schlissel: In the interest of justice, equity and common sense, an award of maintenance should not cause the payer to become destitute. That's where having competent legal representation is crucial. It's the attorney's job to educate the court as to the payer's financial circumstances.

CHILD SUPPORT

Interviewer: You gave a basic percentage amount (depending on the number of children) that someone would be expected to pay. What are some of the major factors that go into child support calculations?

Elliot S. Schlissel: Well, that's just the basic child support and often there are caps. The law provides for it. However, judges will often cap the amount of income subject to child support at between  $250, 000 to $300,000. Over and above the basic child support which is on a percentage basis, the person paying the child support must also contribute a pro rata share for childcare expenses while the other spouse is working.

Over and above that, medical insurance must be provided for the children by one of the parties and the moneyed spouse must contribute to deductibles and coinsurance payments for the children. In addition, the moneyed spouse must contribute to dental or other medical-related expenses not covered by insurance.

How Does Shared Custody Affect Child Support?

Interviewer: How about custody – does that affect the amount of child support? Let's say a husband and wife share custody, and it's three days for one and four days for the other. Would that reduce the amount of child support that would normally be paid?

Elliot S. Schlissel: Shared custody in New York is referred to as joint custody. In New York, even if the spouses have joint custody, one parent will be designated "the residential custodial parent". The non-residential custodial parent must pay child support to the residential custodial parent. The settlement agreement or court orders involved in the case must designate one parent as the residential custodial parent.

Also, for school purposes, it establishes where the child is supposed to be attending school, if the child is attending a publicly financed school.

Parties in negotiations who make settlements out of court can take into consideration the contributions of the other

spouse and vary their child support payments, and they do not have to follow the formula in the Child Support Standards Act.

If you litigate in a court, judges will generally follow the Child Support Standards Act in allocating the child support obligations. With regard to the child support, let's take an example one spouse makes a $100,000 a year and the other spouse makes $50,000 a year. If the spouse that makes $100,000 a year receives custody, the spouse making $50,000 a year still has to pay child support. It's not relevant who makes more money. The nonresidential custodial parent must contribute to the financial needs of the children, i.e. he or she must pay child support to the residential custodial parent.

Interviewer: Do you have scenarios where your client will say, "Hey, my ex is not spending the child support money on the children. they're blowing it on something frivolous"? Can you get amounts amended or taken away?

Elliot S. Schlissel: I have heard this complaint many times. Unfortunately, the child support statute gives the residential custodial parent broad discretion as to how to spend child support payments. The law does not provide that any accounting needs to be given to the person paying the child support as to how the recipient spends the money. However, if the recipient was buying illicit drugs with the money or gambling with the money or doing something else totally inappropriate, that could be brought to a court's attention.

Interviewer: What happens if one of the parties loses a job or they get a better job or circumstances change? Can you get support payments amended?

Elliot S. Schlissel: Let's start with your first example. There is a common misunderstanding in the event you lose your job or you are downsized and you start making less money, your child support obligations automatically change. That is untrue. If you have a court order concerning child support and your financial circumstances change and you're making less money or you're unemployed and making no money whatsoever, you still have to bring a proceeding in either the Family Court or the Supreme Court for a downward modification of child support. You must obtain a court order changing your child support obligation. Only by court order can your obligation be changed.

In a case where income levels have changed, a party to a Family Court order or a divorce who feels the other parent's earning has gone up significantly can bring an application for an upward modification of child support.

REMEDYING UNPAID SUPPORT

Interviewer: If a parent refuses to comply with a child support order, what kinds of remedies are there? What can you do?

Elliot S. Schlissel: There are a variety of remedies for non-payment of child support. To start with, you can have the other parent's wages garnished either by court order or there's a procedure that private attorneys use. You can also bring court proceedings via the Family

Court or the Supreme Court to enforce the child support obligations.

In addition, you can bring, under certain circumstances, contempt proceedings and ask that the other parent be incarcerated for up to six months for failure to follow court orders concerning the payment of child support.

Interviewer: Those remedies sound good. Do they work?

Elliot S. Schlissel: They are powerful remedies. However, the wheels of justice spin slowly. It is sometimes a very time-consuming and frustrating process to effectuate these remedies through the legal system in New York.

Interviewer: What about spousal maintenance? Does it have similar protections?

Elliot S. Schlissel: Yes, there are similar procedures to enforce spousal maintenance awards.

JUDGES' GENDER BIAS

Interviewer: Have you seen favoritism by the courts where a woman will be paid more than a man?

Elliot S. Schlissel: Men often feel they're not treated as fairly as women in divorce cases by Supreme Court judges or by Family Court judges when it comes to matters of custody and support. Women have said the same thing to me

–they don't feel they're being treated fairly. They feel men are able to avoid their responsibility towards them and the children.

Interviewer: If spousal maintenance is required and there is child support, will child support always trump and push down the amount of spousal maintenance?

Elliot S. Schlissel: The way it works in New York, to explain it, I need to give you an example. Let's say the moneyed spouse was making a $100,000 a year. Let's say he or she had to pay $25,000 a year in spousal maintenance alone. For purposes of child support, it would be assumed the moneyed spouse now makes $75,000 a year and the non-moneyed spouse has an income of $25,000 a year. The child support would be paid on a lesser amount based on the $75,000. You receive a deduction for child support before you calculate spousal maintenance.

Temporary Support

Interviewer: So, once a divorce is filed, what if the non-moneyed party has no income of their own and the moneyed spouse cuts them off. How does a person manage? Are there any intermediate measures that can be taken?

Elliot S. Schlissel: Yes. The parties can reach an understanding and their attorneys can work out out-of-court agreements as to an amount that will be paid for child support and spousal support while the action is pending. However, if the parties can't agree, you can bring what's called a "pendente lite application," which is an application made to the court for temporary support during the pendency of the case. The court can make awards covering expenses to the household such as the rent or the mortgage payments, utilities, auto insurance etc. The Court can also award temporary child support and temporary spousal maintenance.

Child Custody

Interviewer: How does child custody work? You said that men fear that the woman in the relationship will be favored, but what happens in reality?

Elliot S. Schlissel: In the Old Testament, there's a story about King Solomon. King Solomon was considered the wisest of the Jewish kings. A situation occurred where two women had children on or about the same time and during the night one of the children died. The babies were lying next to each other. They brought the situation before King Solomon. Both women claimed the baby that died was the other woman's and that the baby that survived was hers.

Solomon told his bodyguard to draw his sword and cut the child in half and give half of the child to each of the women. The bodyguard drew his sword and one of the women threw her body over the child and said, "I lied! Give the child to her. Punish me for lying." Solomon, being the wisest of the Jewish kings, knew only the woman willing to risk her life and surrender her claim to the child was the true mother and deserving to have the child awarded to her. Solomon awarded the child to the mother who risked her own life to save the baby.

Unfortunately, judges in New York do not have this remedy available to them. Custody is the most perplexing and difficult issue judges' face. In family cases, sometimes you have custody disputes where you have two loving and dedicated parents who would each be an excellent custodial parent for the children and this presents a court with a very difficult decision to make.

In other situations, you have cases where one parent has been the primary nurturing parent and who raised the children, took them to doctors, attended school functions, fed them, dressed them, bathed them, and the other parent was only peripherally involved in these everyday tasks. In these cases, custody disputes are easier for judges to resolve.

When there's a custody dispute, the judge appoints an attorney to represent the child or children to take their position into consideration with regard to who should be the residential custodial parent.

Interviewer: How do you interact with that attorney?

Elliot S. Schlissel: Both of the attorneys for the spouses or the parents interact with that attorney as someone who represents a litigating party in the dispute. I have issues sometimes when a young child states a position that was manufactured by one parent or the other by placing a specific point of view in the  child's mind and the attorney for the child doesn't take into consideration the child was manipulated into a point of view.

Interviewer: What is this attorney that represents the children called?

Elliot S. Schlissel: The "attorney for the child".

Interviewer: Does this particular type of attorney have to be assigned to a child?

Elliot S. Schlissel: A judges appoints an attorney for the children when either party requests it or the judge feels it is necessary. If custody is not disputed and there are no significant issues, it is not necessary to appoint an attorney to represent the children. It's usually only done in custody disputes.

Interviewer: How tough are custody disputes?

Elliot S. Schlissel: Sometimes in custody disputes there is a winner and a loser. You cannot cut children in half. Joint custody is usually resolved in out-of-court settlements. In litigated matters, in most cases, if the case goes to a trial and a judge makes a decision, one party gets custody and the other party receives "parenting time," (Visitation).

Interviewer: In a dispute, what are the major factors that, courts tend to take into account? Do they tend to come up with half-and-half arrangements, or do they tend to really skew it more?

Elliot S. Schlissel: Generally speaking, if a case goes to trial, a judge makes a decision that one parent is given custody and the other parent is given parenting time every other weekend, every other holiday, and they also have weekday visits or after-school visits once or twice during the week with the children.

Interviewer: That seems pretty skewed.

Elliot S. Schlissel: When people work out a settlement with private attorneys out of court they can fashion the parenting time in any way they want. Judges, however, generally do not work out very detailed parenting time arrangements. They try to keep them simple so they're easily enforceable.

Interviewer: Definitely sounds like it's in the parties' best interest to try to resolve the child custody/ parenting time issues between themselves?

Elliot S. Schlissel: It is in parties' best interest in all matrimonial and family law matters to try and work out settlements out of court. The courts in New York are overcrowded. There are significant delays. Judges are presented with extremely complicated problems which, impact on the parties' lives over long periods of time. Judges don't have a lot of time allotted to each case. They try to render the best decision under the constraints they're under. It is usually in everyone's best interest to settle matters out of court. Also, it is more cost-effective to settle matters out of court than to litigate in court.

Self-Representation & Choosing an Attorney

Interviewer: Do people always need an attorney to get divorced?

Elliot S. Schlissel: I always recommend a person protect themselves by securing legal representation. Sometimes people feel they can resolve things on their own, but when they get into the nitty-gritty of the matrimonial and family law issues, they find the process is a lot more complicated than they thought. In cases where people try to resolve things on their own, they often resolve them in a way that later proves to be disastrous for them. I've had two particular cases where people tried to work things out on their own and in both cases, after working them out on their own, the wrong parent ended up with custody.

In one of those cases, it took more than $40,000 in legal fees to undo the mistake. We had to set aside a judgment of divorce where one person signed papers – papers that they presumably had read and understood –where they inadvertently gave the other party custody.

Interviewer: It's definitely in the mother or father's best interest to do it right the first time because there can be serious consequences if mistakes are made.

Elliot S. Schlissel: I would not recommend to anyone to try to resolve a divorce or family law issue without consultation with an attorney. Also I would never recommend anyone to try to perform surgery on themselves.

Interviewer: I've seen places that advertise divorces for only $299. How complicated can a divorce be?

Elliot S. Schlissel: I've seen that too. It's interesting because this just covers the filing fees to get the divorce. These places are not run by lawyers and they simply generate boiler plate forms. There is no legal advice given, no legal protection provided. It is not a simple process. There are multiple documents. By definition these boiler plate documents cannot address your specific needs. For example, in a divorce there are a myriad of issues that have to be resolved. Even if you and your estranged spouse agree on everything, you still need to memorialize your agreed terms properly.

There may be issues involving child support, spousal maintenance, pensions, 401(K) s, summer camp, medical insurance, dental insurance, college education, custody, visitation, etc. Who gets the house? When does child support start? When does it end? When does spousal maintenance start? When does it end? There are numerous issues that if not dealt properly with in the divorce documents, will cause heartache and expenses later. A person should avoid a do- it- yourself divorce and seek out an attorney who has extensive experience in handling divorce and family law matters to represent them.

Interviewer: You're saying that when people go cheap it tends to backfire on them?

Elliot S. Schlissel: Yes, in my experience, it often backfires. We have represented clients in numerous cases where people have gone to paralegal paper preparation agencies or who try to prepare documents off software and the Internet, only to find out that what they've done were documents not accepted in New York, were incorrect, didn't apply to them or they left out information regarding important issues that need to be dealt with in the divorce.

Interviewer: How do you suggest people select an attorney when considering divorce?

Elliot S. Schlissel: That's a very good question. Before going into an attorney's office, you should investigate them – either look them up through local bar associations, Google their names or check their websites. You should, upon meeting them, look into the level of experience they have, look into the facilities they have and whether they have adequate staff. How many attorneys, paralegals, and secretaries are in the office? How many cases similar to yours has that attorney handled? What are the results they have had? How are they viewed by other members of the bar and the courts? People should use due diligence before they retain an attorney.

REMEDYING ASSET SABOTAGE

Interviewer: What about if one of the parties starts racking up debt or selling things and trying to get rid of property that belongs to the marital estate? What can you do?

Elliot S. Schlissel: You brought up a number of problems. People who anticipate a divorce sometimes start hiding their assets. In addition, some people who anticipate a divorce start running up credit card bills  and other debt. The courts have ways of dealing with these issues. Debts accumulated during the marriage are subject to equitable distribution the same way that assets are subject to being equitably distributed. Debts are distributed by a court in a litigated case and distributed in a settlement by the parties and their attorneys. There are also remedies involving the subpoena power, discovery actions, taking depositions, obtaining tax returns, credit reports, copies of securities accounts and bank statements to uncover hidden assets so the parties can have a true equitable distribution of the assets.

Interviewer: If there is bad behavior, are there tools to help you to try to stop it on your client's behalf?

Elliot S. Schlissel: There are tools to deal with bad behavior issues. Judges can issue orders of protection and restraining orders.

Personal Statement

Interviewer: What makes you and your office different, unique, and particularly suited to help people that are facing divorce?

Elliot S. Schlissel: I have an office that is consumer-oriented. Our phones are monitored seven days a week, twenty-four hours a day. We take into consideration what our clients are looking to accomplish, their problems and their financial circumstances. We sincerely seek to help our clients by providing them with the highest quality cost efficient legal representation.

Our Law Office has the facilities, the staff, and the experience to provide optimal results, and we often do obtain optimal results for our clients. In addition, my firm has been doing this for more than thirty-five years and we are highly regarded in the legal community, by our peers, judges, and court personnel.

DISCLAIMER

This publication is intended to be informational only. No legal advice is being given, and no attorney-client relationship is intended to be created by reading this material. If you are facing legal issues, whether criminal or civil, seek professional legal counsel to get your questions answered.

Law Office of Elliot S. Schlissel

479 Merrick Road

Lynbrook, NY 11563

(516) 561-6645

(718) 350-2802

Schlissel.law@att.net

www.schlissellawfirm.com